CLASSIC PIANO REPERTOIRE
EDNA MAE BURNAM

8 GREAT PIANO SOLOS

ISBN 978-1-4768-7438-8

WILLIS MUSIC

EXCLUSIVELY DISTRIBUTED BY

HAL•LEONARD®
CORPORATION
7777 W. BLUEMOUND RD. P.O. BOX 13819 MILWAUKEE, WI 53213

Visit Hal Leonard Online at
www.halleonard.com

"EDNA MAE BURNAM was a pioneer in the piano pedagogy publishing field. I was privileged to work with her for many years, and she was an absolute delight. Every time we talked I left the conversation feeling upbeat and happy, and she had that effect on everyone she met. Edna Mae had the most wonderful outlook on life and delighted in helping people learn to make music. Today she is remembered as much for her whimsically titled pieces as she is for the effectiveness of those same pieces in piano studios around the world."

— Kevin Cranley, president and CEO of Willis Music
September 2012

EDNA MAE BURNAM (1907-2007) is best known as the author of the best-selling *A Dozen A Day* books. The technique series with the iconic stick-figure drawings that Burnam drew herself has sold over 30 million copies worldwide. Burnam was born in Sacramento, California and began piano lessons at age 7 with her mother, Armilda Mae Will. She would go on to major in piano at the University of Washington and Chico State College (now California State University at Chico), and ran a successful independent studio for decades. Her long and productive association with Willis Music began when she signed her first royalty contract in 1937. She followed up the success of *A Dozen A Day* with the *Step by Step* piano course, and in her lifetime composed hundreds of imaginative songs and pieces, including several based on observations she made in her travels abroad.

FROM THE PUBLISHERS

The *Classic Piano Repertoire* series includes popular as well as lesser-known pieces from a select group of composers out of the Willis piano archives (established in 1899). This volume features eight wonderful piano solos by Edna Mae Burnam, progressing from early to later elementary. Each piece has been newly engraved and edited with the aim to preserve Burnam's original intent and musical purpose.

CONTENTS

To my dear friend, Judi Sands-Pertel

Two Birds in a Tree

Words and Music by
Edna Mae Burnam

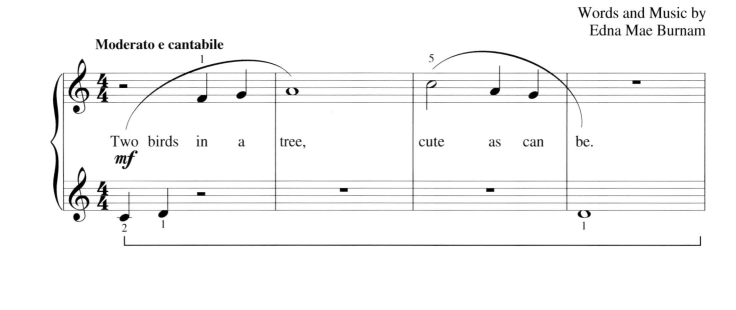

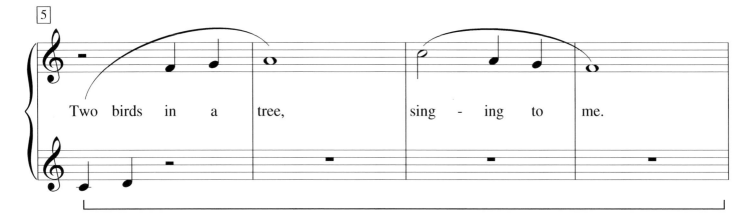

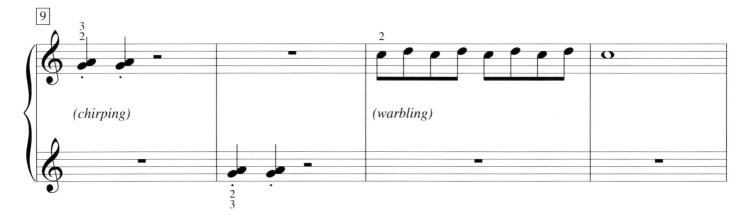

To the teacher: This piece may be learned by note (as written) or by rote (on all black keys in F♯ Major). It is based on the major pentatonic (five-tone) scale F-G-A-C-D, and can be transposed and played easily on all black keys. Pedal marks are suggested.

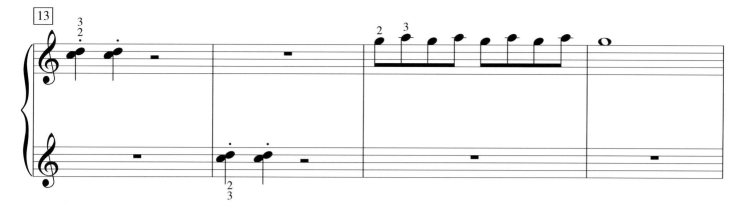

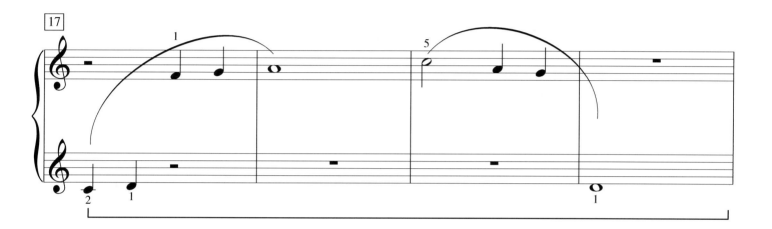

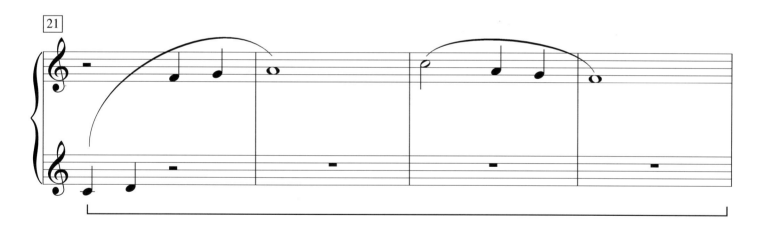

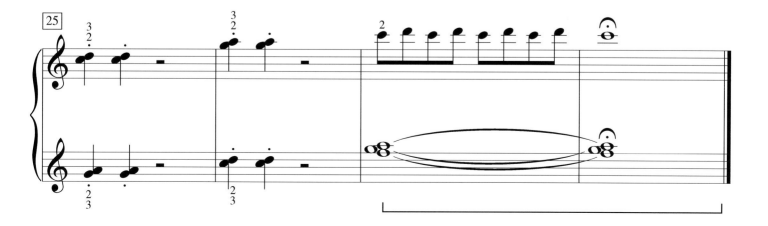

To my grandson, David Bender

The Friendly Spider

Words and Music by
Edna Mae Burnam

Moderately fast

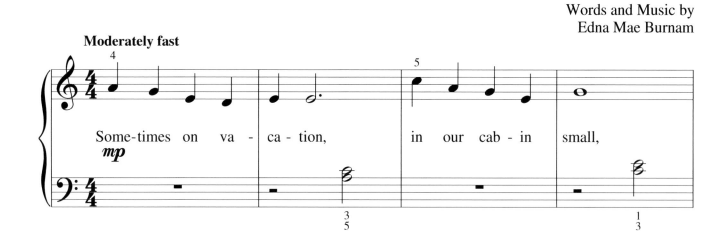

Some-times on va - ca - tion, in our cab - in small,

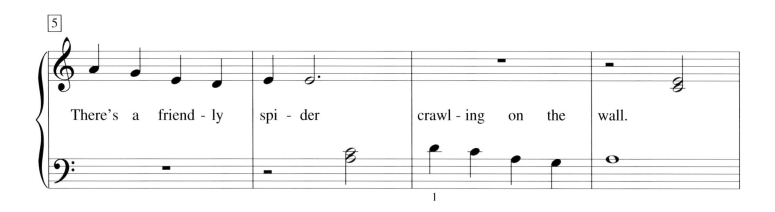

There's a friend - ly spi - der crawl - ing on the wall.

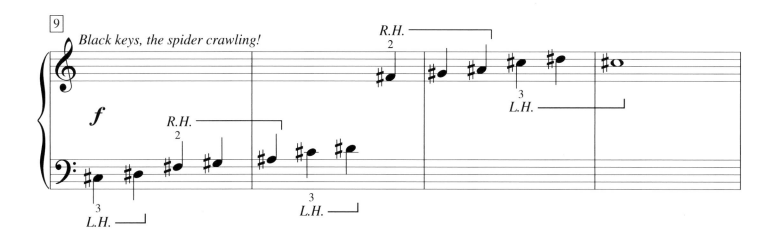

Black keys, the spider crawling!

R.H.

L.H.

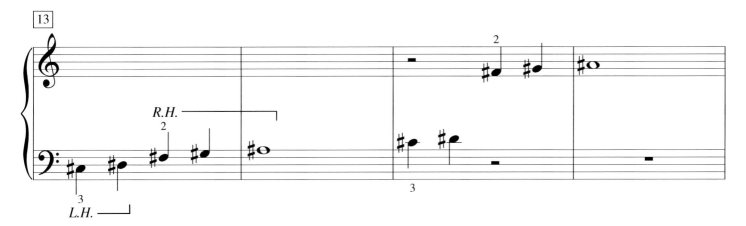

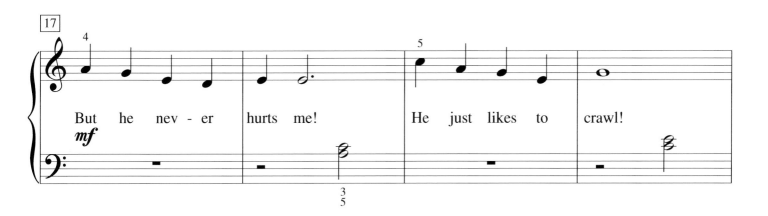

But he nev - er hurts me! He just likes to crawl!

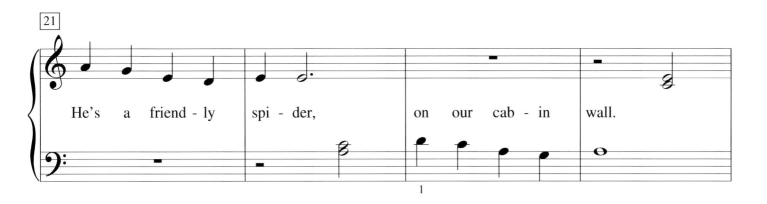

He's a friend - ly spi - der, on our cab - in wall.

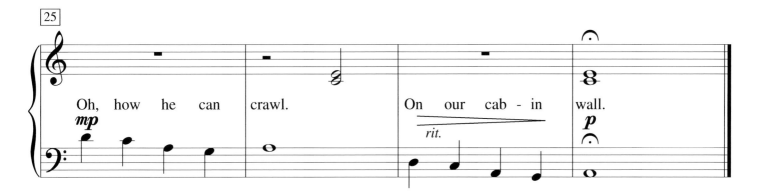

Oh, how he can crawl. On our cab - in wall.

New Shoes

Edna Mae Burnam

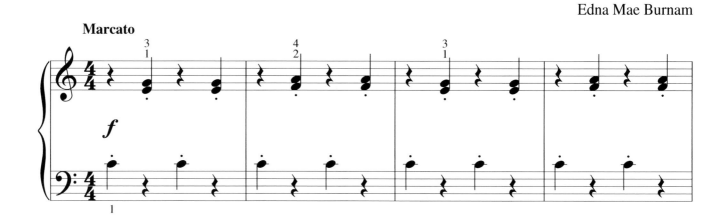

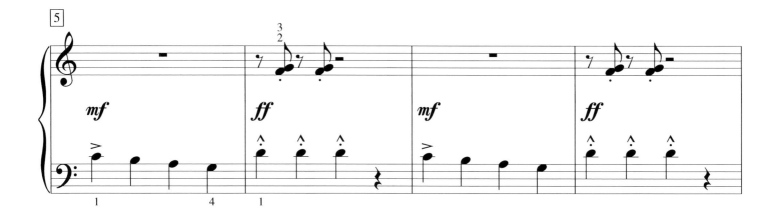

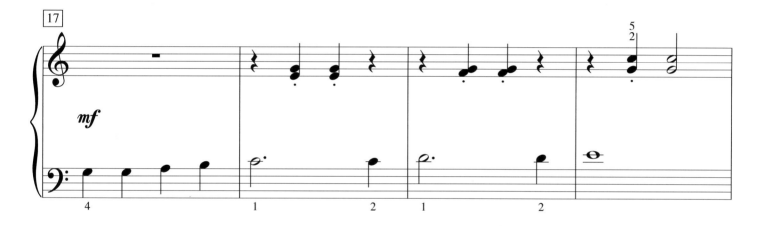

The Clock That Stopped

Edna Mae Burnam

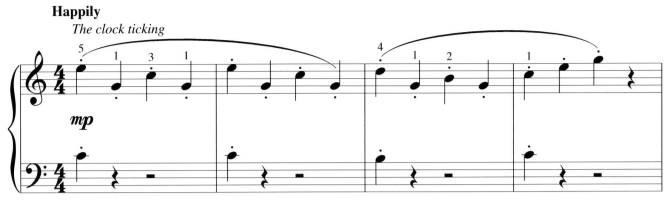

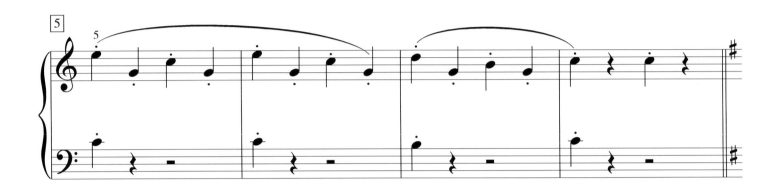

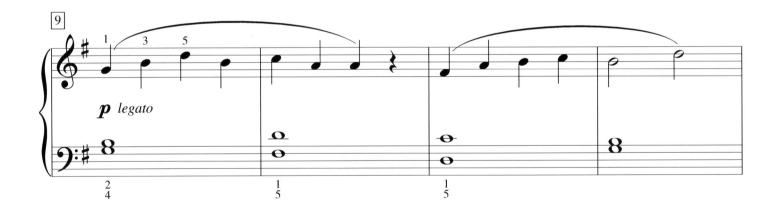

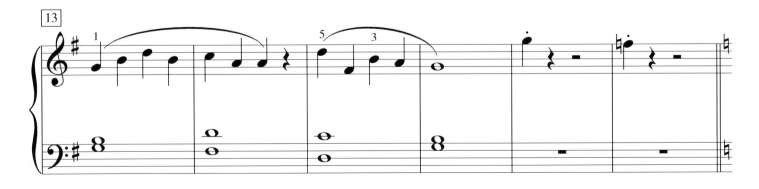

The clock begins to slow down...   *slower...*

loses a tick...   *loses ticks...*   *...The clock stops.*

Winding up the clock...   *The clock ticks again!*

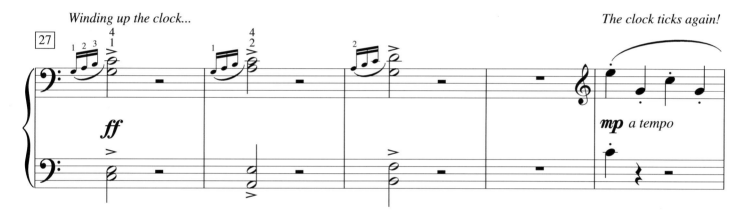

The clock cuckoos three o'clock.

To my dear friend, Mary Tulley

The Singing Mermaid

Edna Mae Burnam

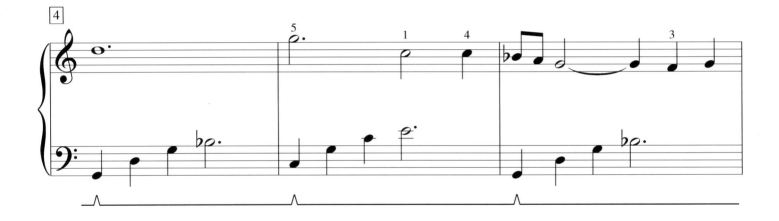

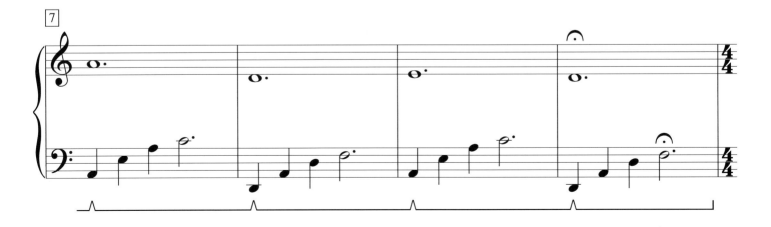

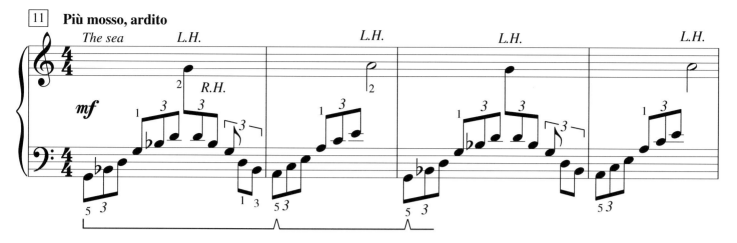

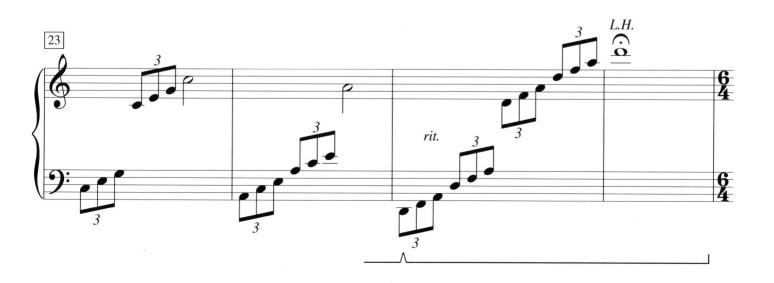

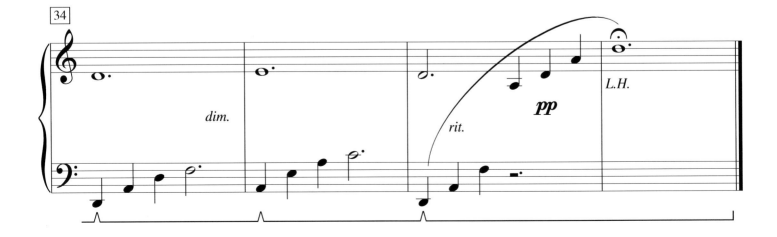

To Chris

A Haunted House

Words and Music by
Edna Mae Burnam

Very spooky!

pp

5 **Rather slowly**

Way out in the coun - try there's a haunt - ed house!

mf

9

Way out in the coun - try there's a haunt - ed house!

13

It is scar - y there! Cob - webs ev - 'ry - where!

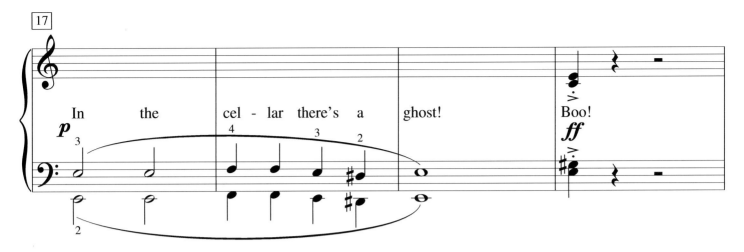

In the cel - lar there's a ghost! Boo!

Way out in the coun - try there's a haunt - ed house!

Way out in the coun - try there's a haunt - ed house!

A little faster

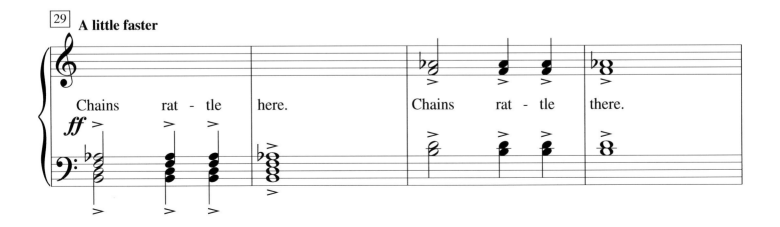

Chains rat - tle here. Chains rat - tle there.

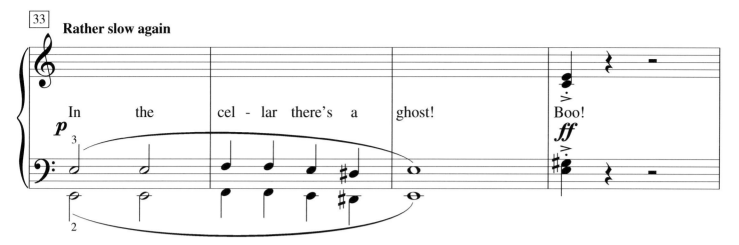

In the cel - lar there's a ghost! Boo!

Way out in the coun - try there's a haunt - ed house!

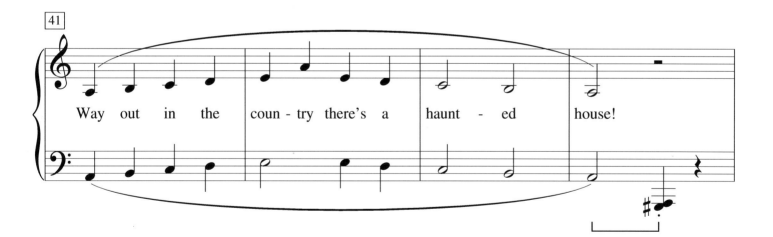

Way out in the coun - try there's a haunt - ed house!

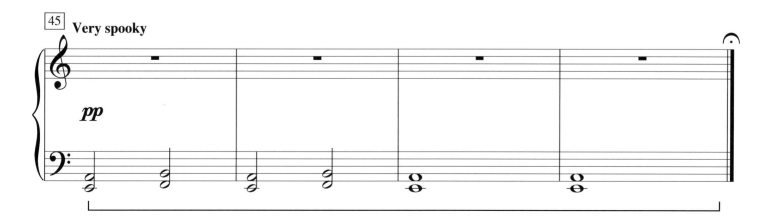

To Mildred Nash

The Singing Cello

Edna Mae Burnam

Moderato, tranquillo

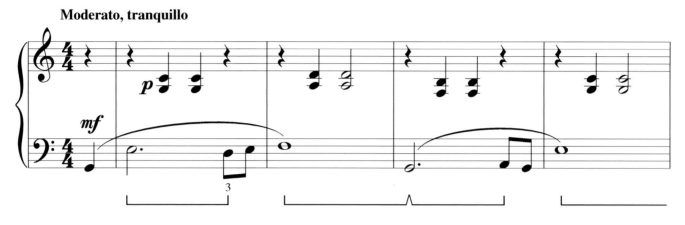

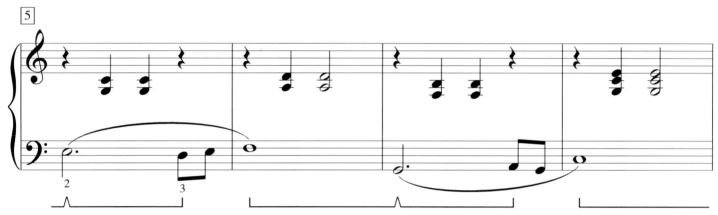

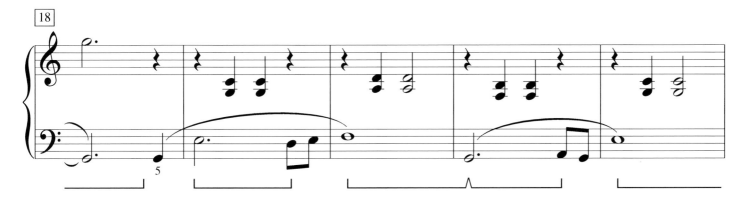

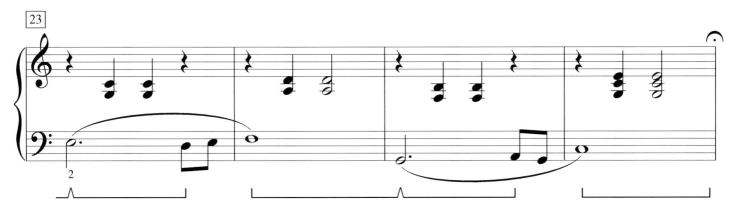

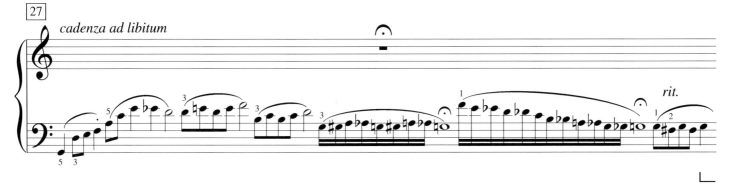

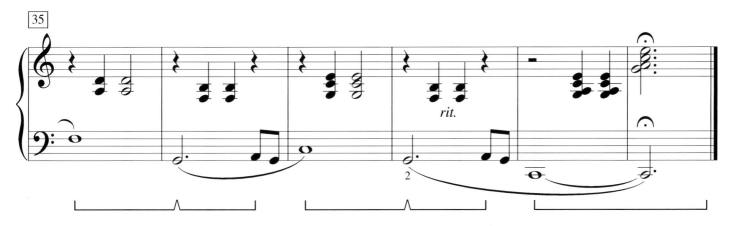

To Esther Benson

The Ride of Paul Revere

Edna Mae Burnam

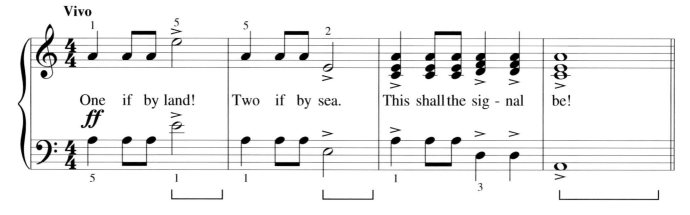

One if by land!   Two if by sea.   This shall the sig - nal   be!

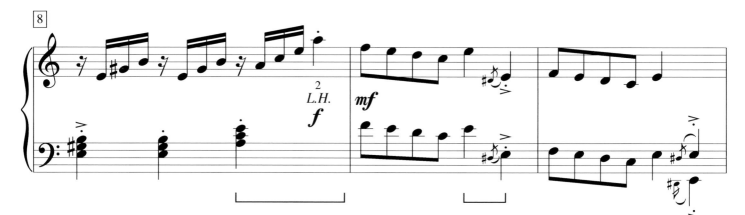

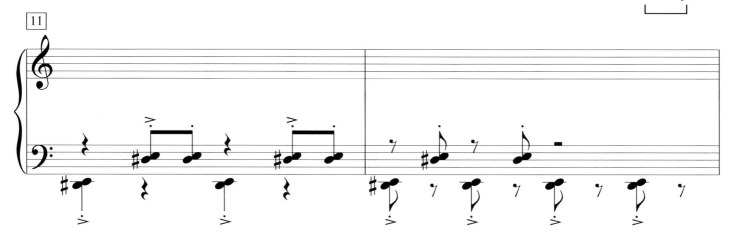

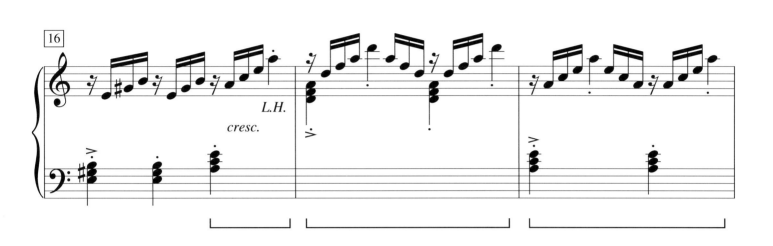

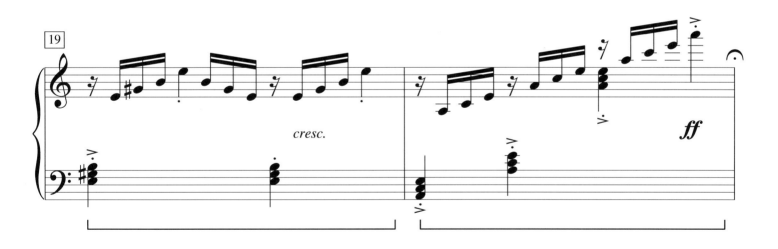

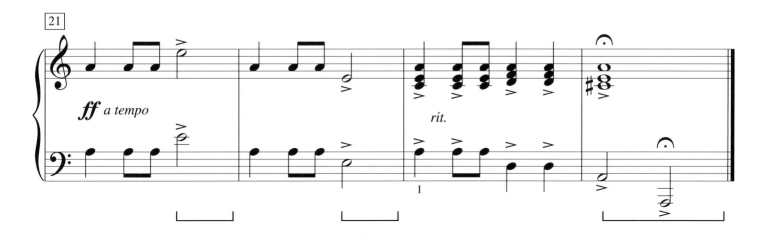

CLASSIC PIANO REPERTOIRE

Classic Piano Repertoire – Edna Mae Burnam
Intermediate to Advanced Level
HL00110229

Butterfly Time

Echoes of Gypsies

Hawaiian Leis

Jubilee!

Longing for Scotland

Lovely Señorita

The Mighty Amazon River

Rumbling Rumba

The Singing Fountain

Song of the Prairie

Storm in the Night

Tempo Tarantelle

The White Cliffs of Dover